Alexandra Kleeberg

You Are Extraordinary

Power Tips for Happy Kids

A Read-Together Book for Small and Tall

With 20 magic exercises and 20 master copies
to color in

I Am So Fantastic Volume 1

'Imagination can achieve everything.' Paracelsus

First edition

© 2017 eVision Publishing, Lindau, Germany

© 2016 of the original German edition Dr. Alexandra Kleeberg, eVision, Lindau, Germany

Images and book cover: Doan Trang (www.doantrang-arts.com)

Email: info@visionpublishing.com

www.evisionpublishing.com, https://www.facebook.com/evisionpublishing

ISBN-13: 978-3-946586-12-8 (English paperback edition)

ISBN-13: 978-3-946586-13-5 (English digital book)

eVision Publishing for Healing and Self-Healing, Potential and Social Development, Germany

Create your vision – Transform your future. Now!

Preface for the adult readers

This book would like to provide a valuable tool for living a creative life for both children and adults: the wand, which is a mighty tool in fantasy.

Right now, scientific research supports the power of creativity. We can revive our imagination to cope with our everyday life, to relive our past and to shape our future.

We can plant the seeds of a fantastic future into the hearts of our children. There we can nurture, fertilize, protect, and watch over them. By encouraging children to present themselves in an authentic way, we liberate our own inner child from the shackles of beliefs and outdated standards. A creative, warm and loving relationship can blossom and development becomes a mutual process.

Parents and children can read this book together. In schools the magic exercises can be integrated into lessons.

This printed version of "You Are Extraordinary" contains an annex with all magic formulas and their related images in full page size to color-in.

This book is the first book of a series of children's books named "I Am So Fantastic". Their intention is to inspire children (as well as grown-ups) to discover the miracle and the might of their body, heart and mind. They learn to influence them and their social contacts by inner images and practical exercises. Thus, they can develop their full potential and well-being.

Preface for the little readers

In this book the butterfly Sophia Monarch, the wise queen of the world of freedom tells the story of her magnificent transformation.

She would like to inspire you, encourage you, guide you and remind you what you are: extraordinary, wonderful and very special. You have got everything inside you that you need to live healthy, happy and magical lives. And when you make friends with all the other extraordinary people - well, then your life really becomes amazing.

Wherever you find the sign with the wand there is a magic tip followed by the ancient magic spell *Abracadabra.*!

Scientists do not know exactly where this magic spell comes from or what it really means - but we know that it works.

The wonderful illustrations by the artist Doan Trang from Vietnam are in black and white so that you can color them in yourself in the printed version, and show how unique and creative you are. Look well after this little book when you have colored it in and you have written in it - so you can look at it again and again when you grow up to always remember how extraordinary, talented, and deeply wonderful you really are.

Enjoy reading,

Alexandra & Dietrich

Table of Contents

Get a free audio-recording of the book by sending an email with your name to info@eVisionPublishing.com

1. Follow your heart

Do you still remember how you used to look dreamily out of the window today?

That is when I fluttered around you very close. I saw how your eyes followed me. I felt your wish to be free and light like me.

So, I took a stroll and flew back to you. 'Do you know that you can carry your life in your hands?' I whispered to you. I felt how your heart opened suddenly just as mine did. Very spontaneously I gave you my wand and laid it gently in the center of your heart. 'Keep it there. Thus, it is always ready for you. The wand is the mightiest tool in your life. With its help, you can change the world with your wishes. The wand will help you to do small and large wonders. So, you will get more and more strong, confident and loving. Just say: *Abracadabra*!'

Magic tip 1

Please imagine that your wand is directly connected with your heart. Then open your heart and let a stream of love flow into your wand. Please send all your wishes for you and your life into this love. Please take care that they are wishes that will make you and all other beings on this planet happy. Please imagine then that all your wishes have already come true. Be happy about your success. Abracadabra!

Magic formula 1: I charge my wand with the love of my heart. I always wish the best for me and for everybody.

2. You have sooooo many talents!

I flew the whole day from one sweet flower to the next. I always thought about you. Therefore, I returned the next evening to your bed. I saw how sweet and blessed you slept. I whispered to you:

Do you know that you are absolutely extraordinary?

Something very special is inside you. You have great ideas and talents that are unique.

They used to call silver coins' people used to pay with in the old days in Europe and the Middle East 'Talents'. Today it is called 'money'.

For me talents are the inner treasures for a happy, healthy, great life.

I grew up in a green, leafy forest. Here you can see all my talents grinning on a lush leaf.

'These are talents?' you asked me in your sleep. 'I cannot buy anything with them! They are just a few eggs…'

'Well, then wait and see what comes out of them. And you may wonder at the end of the book, what wealth these 'eggs' will spread.

To be honest I did not believe that something very beautiful may become of this egg, which I used to be. However, when I look now at these tiny 'talents', it becomes clear to me that something very special has happened to me.

It is the same with you human children – something very magnificent is also sleeping inside of you right now.

3. Your birth certificate

Just like me a lot of talents have been given to you at your birth (given to you as natal gifts). As a visible sign for that I give you your very own birth certificate.

You are wonderful, gifted, talented, unique, magnificent, lovable, free, creative, playful, extraordinary.

Magic tip 2

Please copy your birth certificate and color it in. Fold a copy for your bag, hang one on your wall, on the toilet lid, on a door. Be creative! It is important that you can see it every day. Whenever you pass it, please recite your basic talents out loud. Again and again. Abracadabra!

Magic formula 2: I get to know my natal gifts

4. Find your talents

The birth certificate shows you your general human talents. Please think about them now and sense inside you what your special talents are. I have painted a lot of hearts for you:

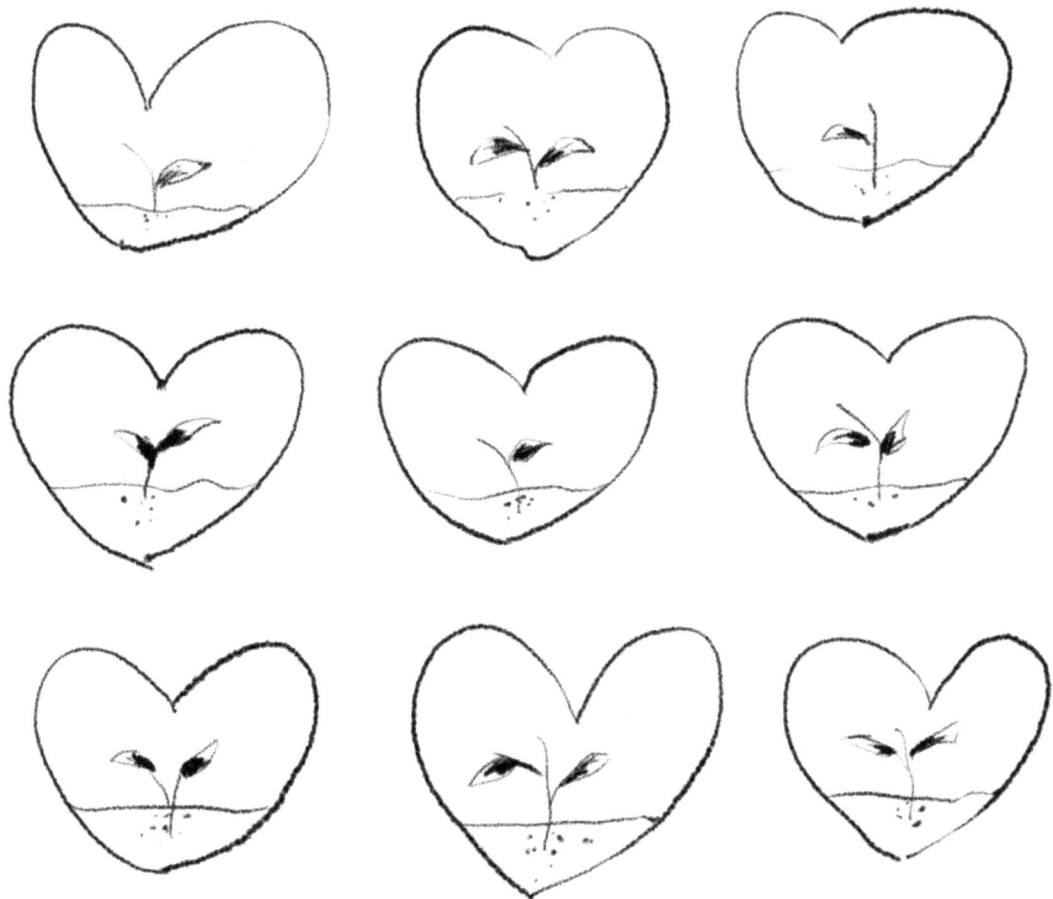

Magic tip 3

Please copy the hearts and write all your talents onto them: what makes you happy, what you are very good at, and what you would like to learn. Then look at all the many filled out (fulfilled) hearts. There the shoots of your wonderful future grow. Please hang the copies of your filled-out hearts next to your birth certificate. Whenever you pass them speak out loud. Abracadabra!

Magic formula 3: I get to know my very special talents and skills.

Then I will also give you a crown. You have really earned it. After all, you are the queen or the king of your life. Don't you think so, too?

Magic tip 4

Please imagine you put a sparkling crown on your head. Your spinal column stretches towards it so that you get quite a bit bigger at the same moment. You balance your crown on your head like a seal with a ball on its nose. So, your spinal column starts to swing and you with it. You know now very deep in your heart that you are the queen or the king of your life. Please wear the crown on your head always. Only at night may you put it beside your bed. Then when you wake up in the morning and open your eyes you can already see how it sparkles. Just put it on when you are on your way to the bathroom. Wear it through the day. Abracadabra!

Magic formula 4: I always wear a (the) crown in the middle of my head.

Magic tip 5

With the crown, you will also receive something else. As soon as you wear the crown on your head, the corners of your mouth will start to lift. They almost reach your crown. Always try to pull them higher and higher and higher. Yes, you shine with a charming smile. Have a look yourself! Abracadabra!

Magic formula 5: I smile at me and my life.

So now you are well equipped for a wonderful life.

I saw that you smiled at me in your sleep. I really fell in love with you then. I felt very close to you. Thus, I started to tell you the story of my life. The story of my big, magnificent transformation. Your smile got wider and wider as I started.

5. Nurture your talents

At that time, as a freshly hatched child, I did not know which talents I had. Yes, even I did not guess my great transformation.

My name is Sophia as you know. But back then, before my big transformation, I was only called 'Oph'. The others simply left out the letters 'S' and 'ia', because I was always so very hungry and just oph – like.

Here you can see me enjoying a fresh green crispy leaf.
You can see that my smile is up to my ears.

Eating was my absolute favorite activity. I enjoyed it though I often burst out of my old clothes. It also did not attract attention, as all my friends were nibbling away and enjoyed the fresh green, too.

For you, as a human child, it is about nurturing your heart and with it your talents, so you can grow, prosper and blossom.

Food for your heart is love, love, love. And now I would like to tell you a secret: The most important thing is that you love yourself. Then you are free and self-determined.

Magic tip 6

And now put yourself in front of the mirror, in front of a glass window, or in front of your own picture every morning and praise yourself for your talents, your special gifts, your very special way of being on this world:

'I am awesome. I am wonderful. I am strong. I am... '
'I love myself. I love myself. I love myself. '

Repeat the sentences aloud, hop, jump, dance with it. 'Abracadabra!'

Magic formula 6: I love me just the way I am.

6. Learn with enthusiasm

A big watering can you can use to
water and fertilize your talents is
called enthusiasm. It is one of your
natal presents, too.

It is so important that learning is
fun for you. With enthusiasm
your brilliant brain bubbles full of
messengers which help you
expand your knowledge and be curious.

Everything else is what people call 'stress'
and this does not really do any good.

So, I have shown you how you can learn
enthusiastically.

You hop and jump and dance with it.
And laugh like I do on my green leaf.

Magic tip 7

*Memorize all your talents while you hop, dance or rage with it
enthusiastically.*

Magic formula 7: I become enthusiastic about myself and my life.

7. Wishes

And then I experienced something magnificent.

One day I crawled to one of these nourishing green leaves that had a small corner of blue light uncovered. Fascinated, I looked up. For the first time, I understood that the world was wider and bigger than my green leaf where I felt at home. I craned my head upward through the green thicket of leaves. The scraps of gold mottled blueness grew. Suddenly I discovered fluttering beings who danced in a bright light. They looked magical as they waved their orange spotted wings. I could hear words buzzing from them.

'You are so extraordinary, there are so many talents sleeping inside of you. You will become something very beautiful one day', one of these winged creatures shouted to me.

A whole swarm of these angels followed her and laughed as they said, 'Yes, you will become very beautiful - just like us. Life is sweet, free and light. You will see it; you will also experience it.'

With this promise they flew away and I got back to my leaf. It was trembling. My head was pounding. Everything wobbled and I felt exhausted and went into a deep sleep.

But the words of the orange colored angels sounded in my dreams. Inside me grew the desire to fly, too. How could this happen? I had no idea, really. And yet - I saw myself flying, swinging widely and freely.

Magic tip

Yes, you also certainly have wishes, desires and goals. I give the hearts to you again - write your wildest dreams on them. Copy the hearts, color them in and hang them up everywhere you pass daily. Yes, there where your birth certificate and all your talents are already hanging. Now your wishes join them, too. Read them aloud every time you pass them as well. Memorize them. Rejoice, hop and dance with it. Abracadabra!

Magic formula 8: I am enthusiastic about my wishes.

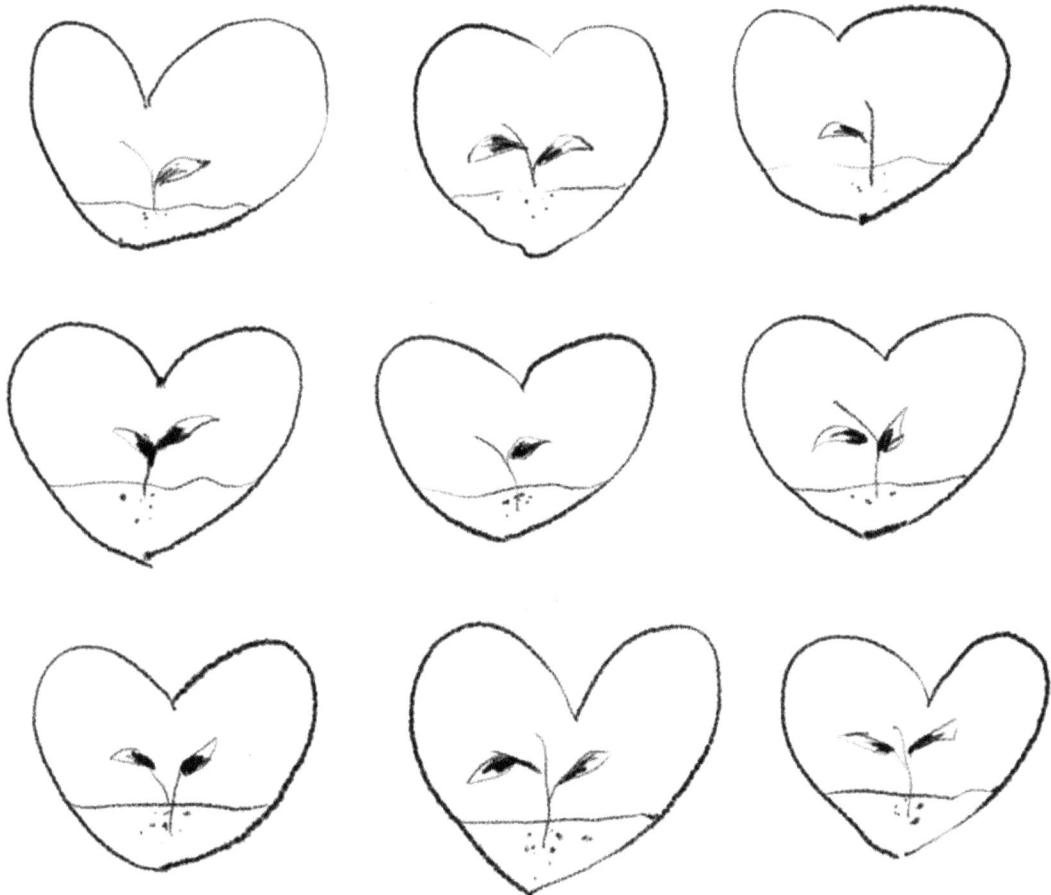

8. Protect yourself!

Suddenly I was nudged. A few very young caterpillars crawled towards me as if they had heard my dream. 'You 're crazy. Do you think you are better than us? Just forget it.'

If somebody puts you down, offends you, or devalues you – please do not allow this to get too close to you or even to get inside you. There is a saying: 'What the person says, is what the person is'. Everything we say is a mirror of our soul. Everything we hear reveals something about the person saying it.

First, I was outraged and I cried out loud. It does not sound so loud when we caterpillars do it, but you human children can cry out very loud to relieve yourself. This is absolutely important, so you can let go of all the tension that is inside of you. Sometimes the adults do not like it so much. However, the wand even has a solution for that.

Magic tip 9

When the coast is clear simply shout out loud. Let go of all your anger, your fear, your tension. If an adult is nearby and you want to remain undiscovered then rage wild - without voice. Or you can swing your wand and imagine that you roar like a lion, you scratch like a cat, you bark like a dog, or you explode like a volcano... just imagine something that relieves you and does you good. Abracadabra!

Magic formula 9: I openly express my feelings.

After letting off steam, I retired. I just wanted to be alone. I kept my desires and my dreams to myself. Then I suddenly felt that I was surrounded by a circle of golden light that protected me. I could use this to keep away other people's insults from me.

Magic tip 10

Please imagine you draw a protective circle around yourself. You can create it with light, with chalk, with colors, with smells. Please invent the best protective circle for you. Sense how you feel secure and at home in it. Dissolve it when you feel secure again. Abracadabra!

Magic formula 10: I conjure a protective circle for me.

I continued nibbling with relish, more than ever. I got bigger and bigger and burst out of my old skin.

9. Dream, dream, dream

I found out that it was
really great to be myself.
The protective circle soon turned
into a protective cover, like a cocoon.
I just wanted to continue to dream –
totally undisturbed.
We caterpillars can do it quite
simply. We search for a branch,
pupate and hang out.

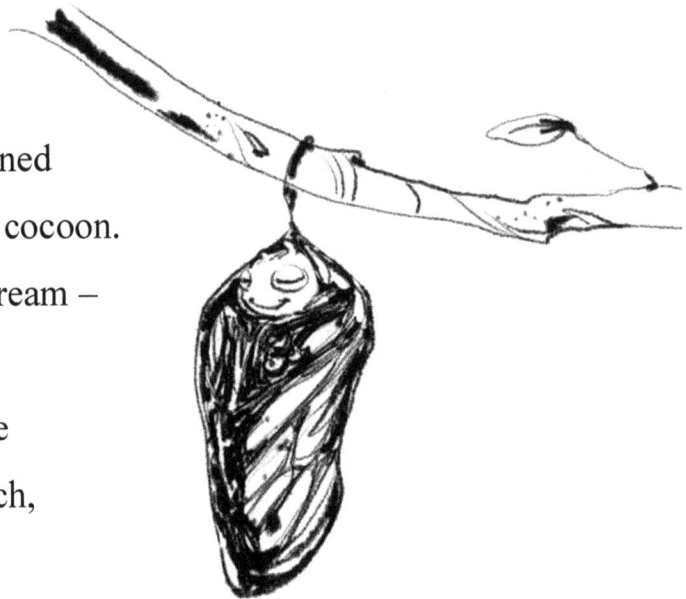

You human beings call this wonderful condition 'taking a time-out'. Or simply even 'hanging out'.

Now and then a gentle wind brought some vibrations, but most of the time I had peace. I swung back and forth and felt loose and easy. I dreamt and dreamt and dreamt.

I dreamt myself into a golden protective covering, secure, free, and at home.

I saw two lions that protected me. I would like to also give you two lions to protect you. They felt so powerful, so at home, and simply incredibly strong.

Wave your magic wand. Invent your own power animals to accompany you. Place them where they are good for you and relax your body. Abracadabra!

Magic formula 11: I conjure power animals to protect me. Abracadabra!

I had the feeling that nobody could do me harm. The two would always protect me, defend me. And I could cuddle with them.

And the dream got even better: the two lions transformed into two angels who protected and comforted me.

And suddenly one of the angels took me between them and I could fly. I flew with them into the sky and got more and more light, free, and buoyant.

Magic tip 12

Wave your wand. Change the power animals into angels who comfort you. Sense how you trust them and how your body is prickling pleasantly. It is great to have your guardian angel with you all the time, isn't it? They always accompany you. Yes, they can even whisper answers in your ear, which encourage you and strengthen you. Imagine that you can fly like they can. Abracadabra!

Magic formula 12: I conjure beings which comfort me.

These dreams were so gigantic that I could forget the insults very quickly!
In fact, I felt bad for the two other caterpillars - what a person says is what
a person is. I could forgive them.

10. Love yourself just in the way you are

One morning it rained and a drop remained on my golden case. Cool and pleasantly moist. At first I wanted to shake it off, but it sparkled so beautifully. I looked at it: in this drop I saw the orange spotted shape of a delicate beauty. It was huddled and hidden behind an almost transparent veil.

Had one of those angelic beings settled down on me? I wanted to talk to it, but it only repeated my questions. I got angry, and kept asking: 'Who are you?' And heard an echo as a reply: 'Who are you?

I looked this creature in the eyes.
Somehow, I knew these eyes.
Something seemed familiar,
yet very strange. And then,
it dawned on me: That's me!
I am beautiful, orange-colored,
and delicate. My heart was
filled with happiness, my body
trembled and burst my shelter.

Do you notice that you can see
yourself more and more in the
way that you really are?
And how you feel love for yourself
more and more?

Magic tip 13

Feel how unique you are. Sense, how lovable you are. Love yourself dearly. Embrace yourself, kiss yourself, caress yourself, praise yourself. Please take time again and again for loving yourself. Abracadabra!

Magic formula 13: I show myself how much I love me.

I wanted to break free.

I shook myself and stretched in all directions. While something amazing happened. In this shaking and pressing process something was squeezed out of me that I could unfold. I realized suddenly, that I was tall and wide. I almost felt weightless. I became aware that something swung inside of me – free and easy. I repeated this new movement. I was sooo proud!

I swung these new wings more and more powerfully and wider.

Magic tip 14

Dare to come out of your cocoon. Yes, come on, present yourself to the world just the way you are. Show your feelings to other people. Open your heart. Become more and more free and light. Abracadabra!

Magic formula 14: I open my heart.

11. Be free

What happened then is simply indescribable. I was sooo happy when I took off for the first time. What a lightness! I felt super, super, super good. The air carried me like a tender cloud.

I can hardly find words for the feeling of happiness that flowed through my body when I took off for the first time.

I only needed to move the wings a little and then they took me forward - out of the leafy thicket. I followed the sun's rays, rising higher and higher.

Magic tip 15

Just go outside - in a meadow, into a forest, or wherever. Jump, hop, romp around. Feel free, light and open. Spread your wings just like that: Abracadabra!

Magic formula 15: *İ conjure me wild and free.*

12. Swing together

I flew over meadows, over fields and streams – I saw the whole world from above.

And then I saw them: these orange winged angels, as they flew from flower to flower. I joined them and was taken up in a warm puffy fluffy welcome.

I was at home now, in the middle of my swarm.

Magic tip 16

Find your swarm, too - those people who like you and whom you like.
Open up. Contact other people in a free, nonchalant and easy way. If this

frightens you, then read in advance through all your talents and your wishes again and again - rejoice, dance, jump full of joy about yourself. Sense inside how wonderful and extraordinary you are. Abracadabra!

Magic formula 16: I conjure friends for me.

Two butterflies, who were golden speckled in a particular way, flew directly to me and said in a way that was happy, shining and full of love: 'We are so very sorry that we insulted you before. We were clueless about the wonder that is possible. But your dream reverberated in secret inside of us and encouraged us. Now we are free and light and you are simply wonderful. Thank you!'

İ was sooo happy! Of course, İ had forgiven them already. So İ learned to love the whole world.

13. Spread the fullness of life

Here, you see me on a blossom where İ drink the sweet nectar of the flowers.

Simply delicious. Each asked me to pass their sweetness on: 'Sophia, please tell the people how infinitely beautiful nature is: colorful, fragrant, creative, and wonderful. The human beings are also children of nature. Tell them that they should listen to their heart – there they will find love, love, love.'

Magic tip 17

Look around and find the talents of other people. Ask them for it. Find out how many many talents there are in this world and imagine all the possibilities that can come of it.

Ask your siblings, your parents, your friends, neighbors, and also your teachers for their talents, wishes and dreams. Be amazed by the many many possibilities. Strengthen them. Sense how people react when you discover their talents.

Please imagine that all people have these seeds in their hearts which can develop in a wonderful way when we water, fertilize and protect them.

Magic formula 17: I am astonished about other peoples' talents.

Then I spread the nectar of the flowers into the world – with every wing beat. And do you know what the next blossom whispered to me? 'I can only reproduce with your help. You spread all my seeds into the world. I thank you. Sophia, in this way you contribute to the spread of beauty, healing powers, and sweet scents. We can only blossom because of you. Thank you. Thank you. Thank you.'

Do you remember how l showed you the grinning caterpillars' eggs that İ called talents? Do you see now how they contribute to the abundance of this world? Without them this splendid abundance would not exist.

Magic tip 18

Give your talents, your joy and your love - they will multiply when you share them. You will get back everything that you give to the world in any way. Even a smile continues flying from mouth to mouth to mouth. Everything you give away will continue to have an effect - deep in the hearts of the people. Abracadabra!

Magic formula 18: I give love.

14. Feel love

This is the story of my great transformation from a little caterpillar to a beautiful butterfly. Amazing, isn't it?

Finally, I would like to give you one last thing.

Do you know that I am in your heart now and forever?

Magic tip 19

Please put your hands on your heart. Can you hear it beat? Please imagine that every heartbeat is like a wing beat. There I swing in a free and puffy, fluffy, light way. So, you can remember me and how wonderful you are. Here in your heart you can connect to everything in a loving way.

Magic formula 19: I feel love for me and all beings.

I am always there for you.

I love you.

Yours,

Sophia

P.S.: Finally, I give you a magnificent picture of your power. Copy it, paint it, hang it up wherever you pass every day. Or shape your very own picture of a wonderful life. Thus, you will always remember that you are unique, lovable and extraordinary.

Magic tip 20

Please imagine that you are always secure, protected, strengthened, free, and deeply loved. Wave your magic wand: So be it, forever! Please imagine how a golden blessing streams through your whole body, your whole life, yes, the whole world. Abracadabra!

Magic formula 20: I conjure a golden blessing for me and interweave it into my wonderful and extraordinary life.

Annex: 20 magic formulas with pictures

Please feel free to copy these pictures for your magic exercises.

Magic formula 1: I charge my wand with the love of my heart. I always wish the best for me and for everybody.

Magic formula 2: I get to know my natal gifts.

GIFTED TALENTED UNIQUE CREATIVE MAGNIFICENT ADORABLE FREE PLAYFUL EXTRA-ORDINARY YOU ARE WONDERFUL

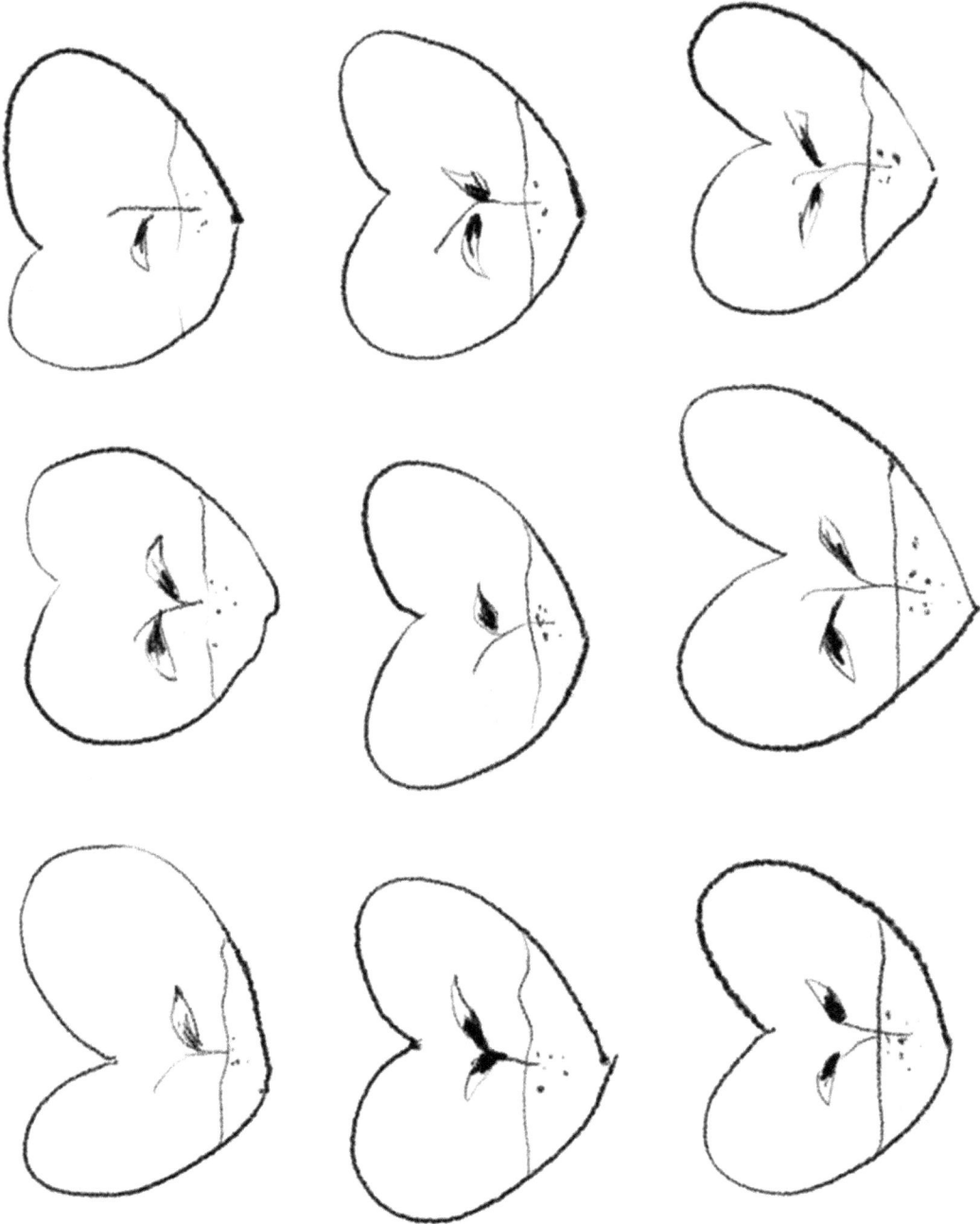

Magic formula 4: I always wear a crown in the middle of my head.

Magic formula 5: I smile at me and my life.

Magic formula 6: I love me just the way I am.

Magic formula 7: I become enthusiastic about myself and my life

Magic formula 8: I am enthusiastic about my wishes.

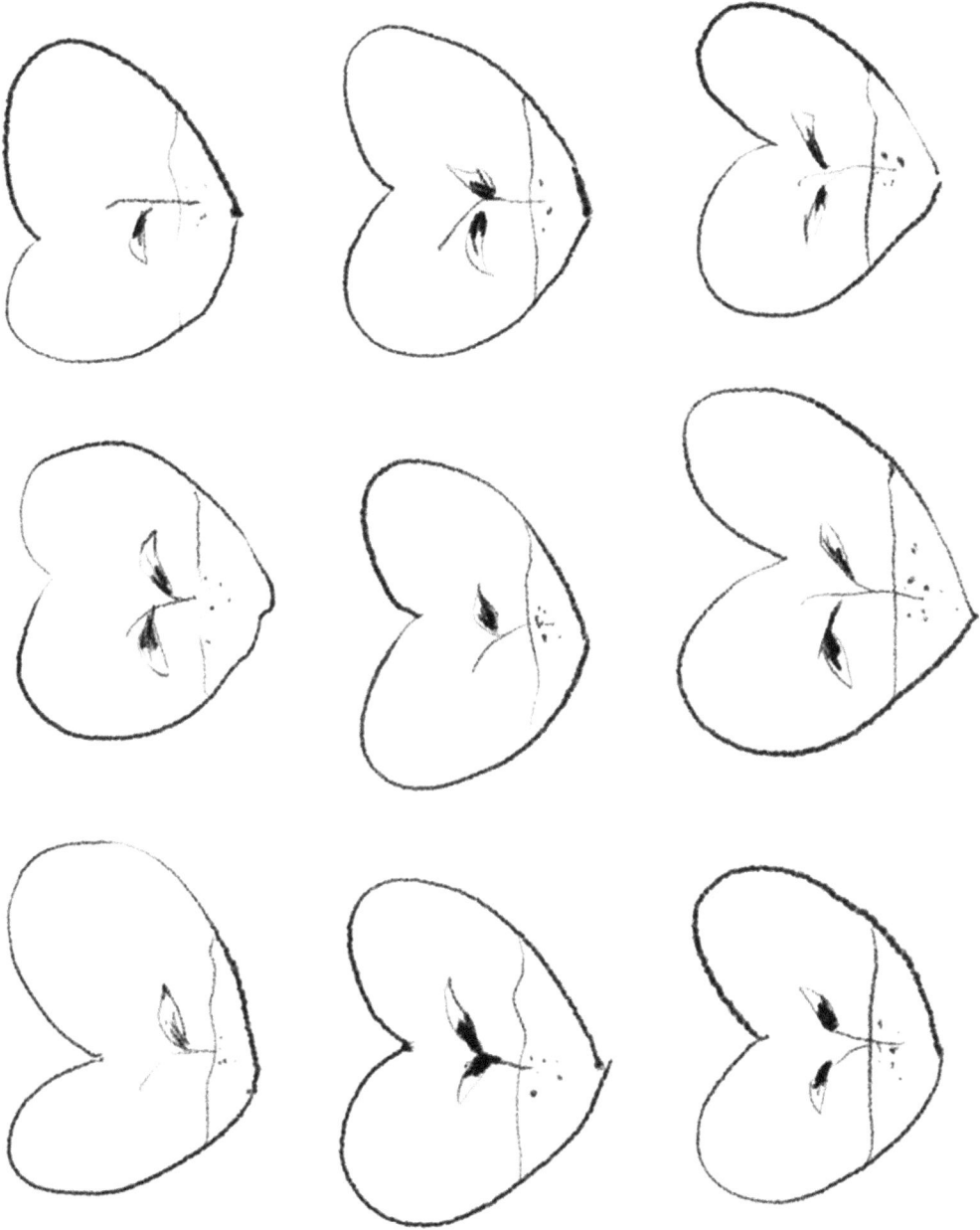

Magic formula 9: I openly express my feelings.

Magic formula 10: I conjure a protective circle for me.

Magic formula 11: I conjure power animals for me, which protect me.

Magic formula 12: I conjure beings which comfort me.

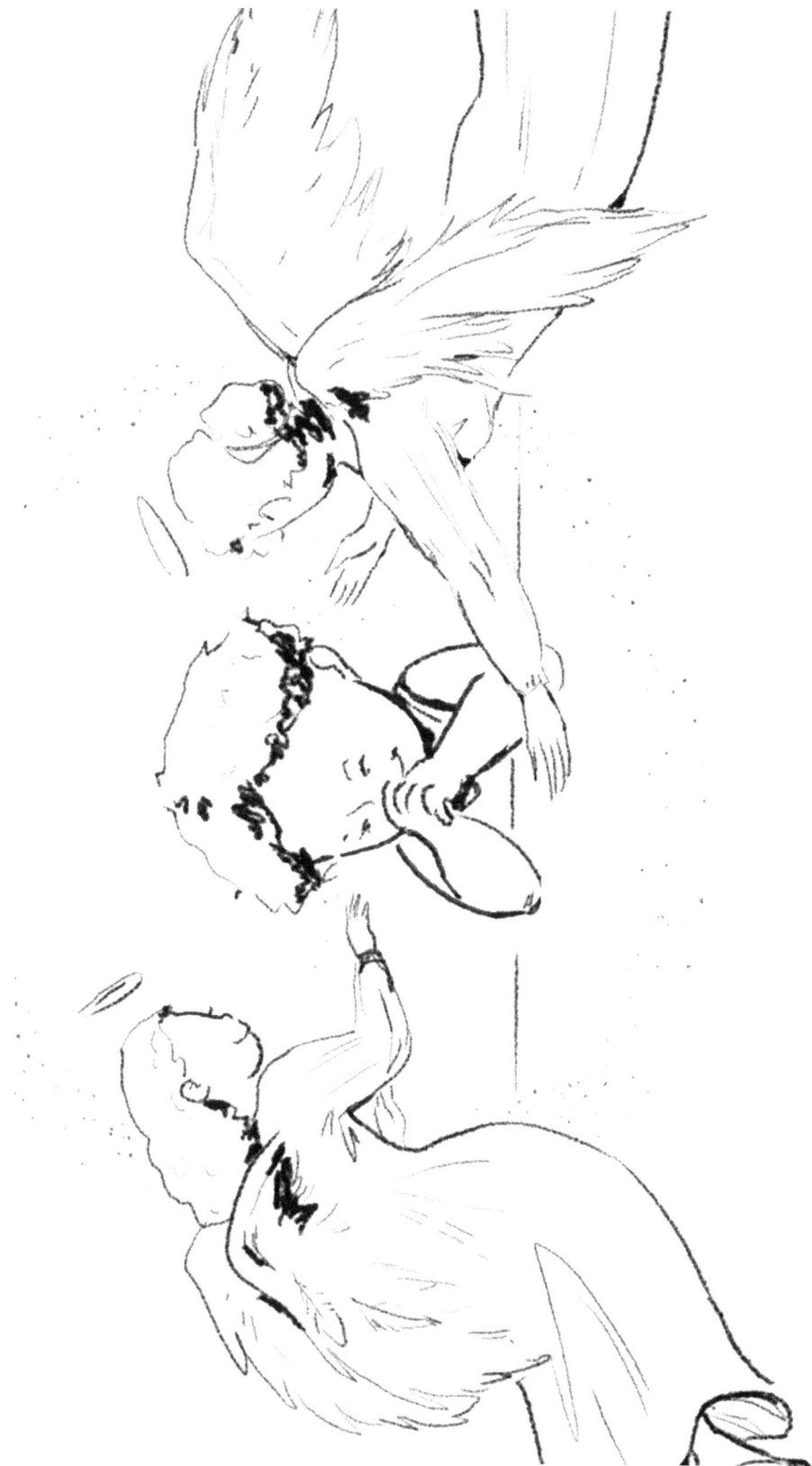

Magic formula 13: I show myself how much I love me.

Magic formula 14: I open my heart.

Magic formula 15: İ conjure me wild and free.

Magic formula 16: I conjure friends for me.

Magic formula 17: I am astonished about other peoples' talents.

Magic formula 18: I give love.

Magic formula 19: I feel love for me and all beings.

Bonus picture: Your wand

eVision

eVision Publishing offers a platform to people who want to share their visions, their tools, their healing and success stories. The vision of **eVision** is the individual and social transformation for a healthy, happy, fulfilled life for all.

With slim electronic and printed books, videos, audios, webinars, seminars and events we want to link and inspire to collect and spread old and new knowledge. Are you enthusiastic about that, too? Visit us on **www.evisionpublishing.com.** Do you have a story to share too?

Wouldn't it be awesome if the power of imagination, which distinguishes us from any other living beings, and which is always with you, would already be taught in schools and kindergartens? Imagine how our children could grow up having no fear any more, understanding the miracles of the functioning of their body, knowing how to heal most diseases, discovering their full potential, developing self-esteem and learning how to lead hearty relations with others.

Our children's books series "I Am So Fantastic" will contribute to make this dream become reality together with people like you. "You Are Extraordinary" is the first Volume of "I Am So Fantastic".

If you like it or have ideas to improve the book, please give us your feedback or a review. To stay in contact, you can join the community of "You Are Extraordinary" on Facebook https://www.facebook.com/You-are-Extraordinary-457334437770107.

For the children's book series, there will also be a website called www.iamsofantastic.com. There you can let us know, which themes for children's books you are interested in.

Create your vision – Transform your future. Now!

T	H	A	N	C	S
R	E	C	E	H	T
A	A	T	T	A	A
N	L		W	N	R
S			O	G	T
F			R	E	
O			K		N
R				T	O
M				H	W
				E	

Alexandra & Dietrich

www.ingramcontent.com/pod-product-compliance
Lightning Source LLC
Chambersburg PA
CBHW081552040426
42448CB00016B/3303